MINDFULNESS AND NATURE

PRISCILLA AN

childsworld.com

The Child's World®
childsworld.com

Published by The Child's World®
800-599-READ · www.childsworld.com

Photography Credits
Photographs ©: Anna Stills/iStockphoto, cover, 1, 6–7, 8, 10,
13; Vera Petrunina/Shutterstock Images, 3; iStockphoto,
4–5, 22; Ann Kot/Shutterstock Images, 15, 16, 20; Karen
Hogan/Shutterstock Images, 18–19

ISBN Information
9781503869653 (Reinforced Library Binding)
9781503880849 (Portable Document Format)
9781503882157 (Online Multi-user eBook)
9781503883468 (Electronic Publication)
9781645498599 (Paperback)

LCCN 2022951197

Printed in the United States of America

Priscilla An is a children's book editor and author. She lives in Minnesota with her rabbit and likes to practice mindfulness through yoga.

TABLE OF CONTENTS

WHAT IS MINDFULNESS?

Sometimes life gets loud. Thoughts and emotions can feel **overwhelming**. The sounds of cars and people talking might feel like too much. Being in nature can help people quiet their minds. This is a kind of mindfulness. Mindfulness is when people notice their thoughts, feelings, and surroundings. Practicing mindfulness in nature helps people slow down. They can feel calmer. People can see, feel, and hear things they never noticed before.

Spending time in nature can help people feel calm.

LISTENING TO NATURE

For spring break, Gabriel's family is camping in the mountains for three days. Gabriel is **disappointed**. A lot of his friends are going to fun places. They are traveling to other countries, staying at hotels, or swimming in pools. Being with his parents is nice. But Gabriel wants to go somewhere fun, too. Now he is stuck in the middle of nowhere. There is no internet. There is not even a bathroom!

Camping can be a fun activity to do with family.

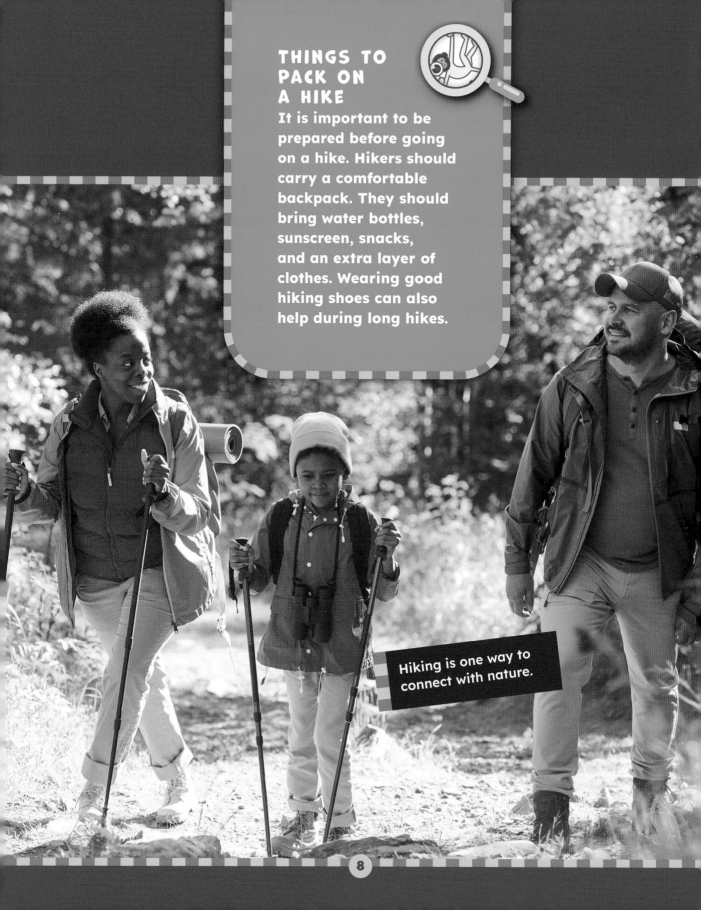

THINGS TO PACK ON A HIKE

It is important to be prepared before going on a hike. Hikers should carry a comfortable backpack. They should bring water bottles, sunscreen, snacks, and an extra layer of clothes. Wearing good hiking shoes can also help during long hikes.

Hiking is one way to connect with nature.

After Gabriel and his parents finish eating lunch, they prepare to go on a hike. Gabriel's mom brings extra snacks and water. His dad gives him binoculars. He says Gabriel might be able to see animals or cool birds.

Gabriel and his parents hike for what seems like hours. Gabriel's feet start to hurt. The sun is shining in his eyes. There are bugs flying everywhere. Sweat drips down his face. Gabriel starts to feel **frustrated**. If they had gone to a hotel instead, he would not be having such a hard time.

"Hey Gabriel," his dad says. "Do you want to take a break? You look tired." Gabriel nods. He and his parents stop and drink from their water bottles. Gabriel sits on the ground.

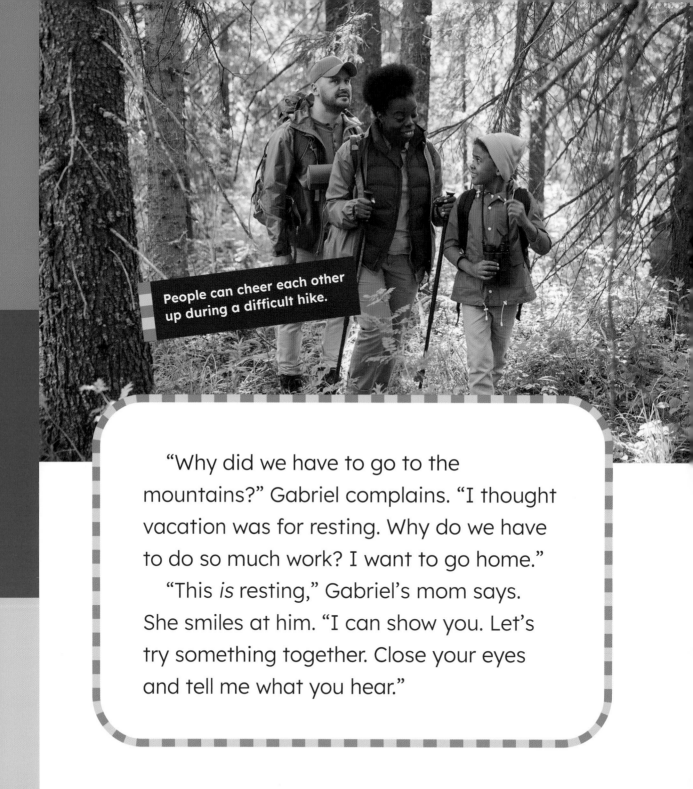

People can cheer each other up during a difficult hike.

"Why did we have to go to the mountains?" Gabriel complains. "I thought vacation was for resting. Why do we have to do so much work? I want to go home."

"This *is* resting," Gabriel's mom says. She smiles at him. "I can show you. Let's try something together. Close your eyes and tell me what you hear."

Gabriel closes his eyes. It helps him pay more attention to the sounds around him. There is so much he did not notice before! The trees rustle in the wind. Birds are chirping. And something is gurgling. It sounds like water. Gabriel opens his eyes. "Is there a river here? I think I hear water."

His mom laughs. "Yes, there is! It's right behind you." Gabriel turns around and gasps. There is a tiny stream in between the rocks. Gabriel reaches out to touch the water. He pulls his hand back in shock. It is ice cold! Gabriel splashes his face with water. It feels so good!

Closing his eyes even for a few seconds helped Gabriel understand that nature makes many wonderful sounds. Before, his thoughts were louder than the flowing stream. But practicing mindfulness helped him **focus** on the things around him. He decides to pay closer attention to his surroundings.

Gabriel suddenly sees a red streak. A bird flies to a tree branch.

"I think that's a woodpecker," his dad whispers. "Use your binoculars. Maybe you can see it better."

Gabriel slowly lifts his binoculars. When he **adjusts** the lenses, he sees the bird. The red feathers on its head makes it seem like the bird is wearing a hat. The woodpecker's sharp beak starts to peck the wood. It sounds like a drumroll. "Wow," he whispers. Nature is pretty awesome!

Binoculars help people see things that are far away.

CHAPTER 3

MINDFUL LIKE A HARE

Sophie hates winter. It is cold and wet. The sky is almost always gray. Today, her **siblings** are sledding on a nearby hill. Sophie stayed home. She did not want to be cold. But she feels lonely being the only one inside.

Sophie's mom is making hot cocoa and gingerbread cookies. She asks Sophie to tell her siblings to come home. Sophie puts on her coat, gloves, and hat. She laces up her boots. When she opens the door, a cold gust of wind greets her. Sophie decides that she will run to the hill.

It is important to wear warm clothes when it is snowing.

WINTER MINDFULNESS

Being stuck at home when it is cold or rainy can be tough. But there are fun ways to practice mindfulness inside. Coloring, doing a puzzle, or even just looking out the window can be mindful practices. When doing these activities, a person can bring her attention to the present. When her mind wanders, she can use the colored pencil, puzzle, or outdoor sights to bring her back to the present moment.

Falling in the snow can hurt.

The sooner she gets there, the sooner she can come back to her warm house.

While she is running, Sophie trips over a rock and falls. Snow gets all over her face and body. Her face is cold and **numb**. Snow gets into her boots and makes her socks wet. Her knees hurt. Sophie starts to cry.

Suddenly, Sophie hears something in the trees. She freezes. She spots something white and fluffy jumping in the snow. Its ears are long and poking up in the air. It is a **hare**. It almost blends in with the snow.

The hare pops its head up in the air. Its wide eyes look toward Sophie and blink. Sophie gasps. She tries to move closer. With each step, her breath slows. The snow seems to fall more slowly. She feels like she is in a different world.

Sophie focuses her gaze on the hare, hoping it does not go away. She sits on the cold snow to watch the animal. She sees it sniffing the air. Its ears move with every small sound. A pile of snow falls from one of the tree branches. The hare hops away.

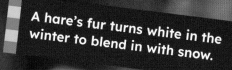

A hare's fur turns white in the winter to blend in with snow.

Even after the hare disappears, Sophie stays and watches the snow come down. She looks at the snowflakes that fall on her gloves. Each one has a different pattern. When she **exhales**, misty clouds leave her mouth. Everything seems so beautiful. She does not even mind the cold!

Sophie hears people laughing in the distance. It is the sound of her siblings. She almost forgot her task of calling them home! Being mindful of the nature surrounding her helped Sophie be more open-minded about winter. Maybe the snow was not so bad after all!

WONDER MORE

Wondering about New Information

How much did you know about practicing mindfulness in nature before reading this book? What new information did you learn? Write down three facts that this book taught you. Was the new information surprising? Why or why not?

Wondering How It Matters

What is one way being mindful in nature relates to your life? How do you think being mindful in nature relates to other kids' lives?

Wondering Why

Focusing on your five senses can be a great way to practice mindfulness in nature. Why do you think it is important to focus on your five senses? How might doing this be helpful to you?

Ways to Keep Wondering

Learning about mindfulness in nature can be a complex topic. After reading this book, what questions do you have about it? What can you do to learn more about mindfulness?

CLOUD MEDITATION

People do not always need to travel far away to practice mindfulness in nature. Nature is always somewhere close. Sometimes, you just need to look up!

1 Go outside and find a comfortable place to look up at the sky. If it is raining, you can stay inside and find a window.

2 Take a deep breath. Look at the sky. What colors do you see?

3 Bring your attention to the clouds in the sky. Are there a lot of clouds? What shapes can you see in the clouds? Are the clouds moving?

4 If you have any thoughts that are bothering you, imagine them going into the sky. Focus on the clouds and on your breathing.

GLOSSARY

adjusts (uh-JUHSTS) When someone adjusts something, he is making changes so it works better. Gabriel adjusts his binoculars until he can see clearly.

disappointed (diss-uh-POYN-ted) To be disappointed is to feel sad because something did not happen as expected. Gabriel was disappointed when his family went camping.

exhales (eks-HAYLZ) When a person exhales, she is breathing out. Sophie notices her misty breath when she exhales in the cold.

focus (FOH-kuss) To focus is to pay special attention to something. Closing his eyes helps Gabriel focus on the sounds around him.

frustrated (FRUH-stray-ted) To be frustrated is to be annoyed or angry. When Gabriel went hiking, he was frustrated with the heat and the bugs.

hare (HAYR) A hare is a mammal that is related to a rabbit but is larger, has bigger ears, and has longer legs. Sophie saw a white hare in the snow.

numb (NUHM) When something is numb, it has no feeling. Sophie's face starts to feel numb because of the cold.

overwhelming (oh-vur-WELL-ming) When a thought or feeling becomes too much, it can be overwhelming. Being in nature can help when thoughts feel too overwhelming.

siblings (SIH-blings) Siblings are people who share a parent or parents, such as brothers and sisters. Sophie's mom sent her to call her siblings back home.

FIND OUT MORE

In the Library

An, Priscilla. *Mindfulness and Pets*.
Parker, CO: The Child's World, 2024.

Kinder, Wynne. *Calm: Mindfulness for Kids*.
New York, NY: DK Publishing, 2019.

Lawler, Jean C. *Experience Nature: How Time Outside Makes You Feel*. Egremont, MA: Red Chair Press, 2019.

On the Web

Visit our website for links about mindfulness and nature:

childsworld.com/links

Note to Parents, Caregivers, Teachers, and Librarians: We routinely verify our Web links to make sure they are safe and active sites. So encourage your readers to check them out!

■■■■■■■■■■■■■■■■■■■■■■■■■■■■■■■■

INDEX